Over thirty years ago, New Mexico Men's Wellness sponsored the publication of a men's poetry anthology, *Talking from the Heart*. Now, *A Wind Blows Through Us*, celebrates that first collection as well as the beauty and promise of the current male experience. As was said in the first anthology "Each poem is a glimpse into the rich interior life of the man who wrote it. We believe that the avenues leading to healing and reconciliation, to redefinition and harmony, are revealed in the mysteries of poetic language. Each poem is a message sent from one human heart to another. Each is a celebration of the human capacity for growth." The contributors to this anthology continue to illustrate this depth and richness.

Hank Blackwell

Out of men's groups meeting throughout New Mexico, several annual conferences at Ghost Ranch, and other venues emerged the first anthology of New Mexico men's poetry: *Talking from the Heart*, published in 1990. This second anthology explores the full range of men's minds, hearts, and spirits. Poetry is uniquely suited for exploring the hidden cellars as well as the celestial mansions of the male psyche–as well as the ordinary humdrum of everyday life.

David Johnson, Professor Emeritus,
University of New Mexico

The stories and visions of this selection of works by New Mexico poets have given us a healthy cross section of the curious minds of men in a New Mexico landscape. The paths we follow on reading this anthology lead us through a journey of fancy and insight that are unexpected and at times profound. I would regard the selection as part of an ever-changing measure of men's creativity from the great, American Southwest.

Raymond Johnson, author of
Swoosh of Heron Wings and other works

Mercury HeartLink
www.heartlink.com

A WIND BLOWS THROUGH US

A Festival of New Mexico Men's Poetry

A WIND BLOWS THROUGH US

A Festival of New Mexico Men's Poetry

EDITED BY

HANK BLACKWELL

DAVID JOHNSON

RAYMOND JOHNSON

Mercury HeartLink

Berry —
Thank you, dear friend, for your wonderful
support of this project and for your continued
friendship —

Blessings,
Hank

A Wind Blows Through Us, A Festival of New Mexico Men's Poetry
Copyright ©2021 NM Men's Wellness Anthology

ISBN: 9781949652116_20-00
Publisher: Mercury HeartLink
Silver City, New Mexico
Printed in the United States of America

Front Cover image by Joseph Woods and Kris Thoeni
Back Cover image by Joseph Woods and Kris Thoeni
Gravel and Grit photo by Uwe Schroeter
Joy and Laughter image by Joseph woods and Kris Thoeni
The Uninvited Image image by Tim Burns
I Grow Old photo by Uwe Schroeter
Be Gentle, Be Kind, Be Strong photo by Roger Harmon
The Road Ahead photo by Uwe Schroeter
Photo of David Johnson and Raymond Johnson by Hank Blackwell
Cover and layout design: Denise Weaver Ross
© 2005-2021 all cover and interior images by Joseph Woods and Kris Thoeni.
Used with permission.

Mercury HeartLink: consult@heartlink.com

Mercury HeartLink
www.heartlink.com

In the off season, I dream
of writing poems—some like
white birds, some like parrots,
their wings in the long night feather
the air with mellifluous sounds.

Chuck Cockelreas
"When the Poems Are Gone"

CONTENTS

I Grow Old

Be Gentle, Be Kind, Be Strong

The Road Ahead

DEDICATON

To the many men who strive to be gentle, kind, and strong.

ACKNOWLEDGEMENTS

Michael Ball
"Big, Loud Toys"
Spillwords, 2020

Hank Blackwell
"Bear", *"Current"*, *"Familiar Face"*, *"Old Dog"*, *"Oh"*, *"River Stones"*, *"Wren"*
Silver Chain, Mercury HeartLink, 2021

Jim Brown
"Rose's Kitchen", "Raven Etiquette"
Language Be My Bronco: A Life in Poems, Psychosynthesis Press, 2012

Raymond Johnson
"Cyclic Move", "Encounter", "En Route", "Goodbye", "Homeless",
"Lathandria", "Manhattan", "Waterbird"
Swoosh of Heron Wings, Duende Press, 2017

Levi Romero
"Years After My Father Died"
Sagrado: Photopoetics Across the Chicano Heartland, UNM Press 2013
"Something About My Father"
In the Gathering of Silence, West End Press, 1996

Stewart S. Warren
"The Unfailing Freefall", "The Unfinished Road"
Feeling the Distance, Poetry Playhouse Publications, 2020

FOREWARD

New Mexico Men's Wellness (NMMW) is one of the oldest Men's Wellness organizations in the U.S. Throughout its thirty-six-year history, this all-volunteer organization has been committed to nurturing wellness in body, mind, and spirit through the sharing of life experiences across generations and cultures in safe, collaborative settings. Conferences, gatherings, volunteerism, and creativity are a few of the products of this incredible organization.

Over thirty years ago, NMMW supported the publication of an anthology of men's poetry. It has done so again, supporting and funding this publication.

Heartfelt thanks to NMMW, its Board of Directors, membership, and volunteers. Sincere gratitude to our contributors-poets, artists, photographers, designers, and publishers for the collaborative creativity resulting in this anthology.

A special thank you and bow to poets, friends and gentle men David Johnson and Ray Johnson for their expertise, artist's eye, cooperation, patience, and heart space that moved this project into a splendid collection. May we all continue to connect, share, support, and always strive to become our best, together.

Hank Blackwell

INTRODUCTION

Over three decades ago, New Mexico Men's Wellness supported the publication of *Talking from the Heart; An Anthology of Men's Poetry*. This collection of poetry, primarily from the men of New Mexico, celebrated the richness of men's creativity, emotions, vulnerability, and interpretations of the world around them. It encouraged men to speak as knowledgeable and sensitive human beings.

Now, *A Wind Blows Through Us: A Festival of New Mexico Men's Poetry*, celebrates over thirty years of this creativity and sharing. One might refer to this publication as one that pays attention to the inner landscape of men's lives, as well as interpreting nature and society. The poet, risking some, perhaps risking all, incorporates this mindfulness with the vulnerability of feeling, in order to recognize and observe the uninvited image and, in fleeting moments, illustrate that moment with language.

To our contributors, we are most grateful for your participation and generosity. To all those who participated, thank you for reminding us of the reach of our circle and that it is always big enough. To our readers, may these offerings encourage your own creativity, your own voice and remind you that when the gift of an uninvited image or experience appears, it is well worth the attention. May these offerings continue to be messages sent from one human being to another.

*For your own peace of mind, don't count
on my favor. And don't badger. Take
solace, if any's to be taken, in my honesty,
which is absolute and irrevocable.*

Chuck Cockelreas

GRAVEL AND GRIT

Cilantro Grin
Mike Ball

The hug of royal-purple comforter
did not comfort. Neil was past caring.
Sneaky late sunlight striped tonight's deathbed.
We bore grief like myrrh into the bedroom.

He breathed but barely, shallow and rapid,
a tired runner with the race ending.
On what would shortly be his final bed,
bucking bronchi spat low barks of soon doom.

Motionless, then voiceless, his presence turned
visitors stupid as stammering drunks.
Often loud, he had loved parlor theater.
AIDS whittled his torso and stole his shouts.

Delinquent gangs of disorders travelled
with and in him, harrying and tugging
as pack predators would a weakened deer.
Insatiable demons chomped all of him.

His Italian blood came with short-lived rage,
and he would sing just the right aria.
He adored the erose leaves, sight, and taste
and yes, peculiar scent of cilantro.

I brought his sort of posy from my pots.
As the clump of cilantro neared his nose,
he then inhaled deeply, coughed faintly,
and grinned, all with now forever closed eyes.

SURFACE
Tim Halford

To live today we are told
Everything can be bought, everyone sold
Compromise is the only way to survive
Don't risk too much, just stay alive!

Alive means food, all that we can eat
romance, heroes, adventures
through a vicarious televised seat.
Media tells us what is "in"
Whom to honor, who is in sin
For a hero today is scapegoat the next
Stick around long enough
You too will be in that text.

No new frontiers, no clear cause
America is bleeding with not enough gauze
Wise old mentors are disposed and forgotten
Young men left floundering; guidance unbegotten.

I seek a cause larger than me,
A spoke, not the cog, in a wheel that spins free
Where risk, even death cards, could be dealt
No compromises, no deals, only what's felt.

With a lover and warrioress near by my side,
Hand in hand, eyes to eyes
No shame, no fear, nothing to hide,
Learning together, growing more wise.

I know that I, too, shall someday die,
My fear is to find no cause, no true love,
Going through the motions, living a lie,
Not letting the Divine give me a free-fall shove.

My soul presses onward, sometimes crying
For a cause that's true, a love undying
This is my bliss, yet I see not the way
I go through the briars, day after day.

This path I am on is right now for me,
Though hard to accept, so much fog I can't see
No grail to seek, no pure cause that is right
I trudge in the dark for this is my plight.

One day I will come to my cause in a clearing,
Where I see for miles and have perfect hearing
Others will come on divergent quest trails
We join together, our quest fills our sails.

"After Braveheart, 1996"

Beggars Are Outlawed, But Not Poverty
David Johnson

The voices of children pulled at my arms–small noses
and eyes mattered like thick cream. We had no suburbs
to retreat to.

A mother and child found their way to our steel door,
the black bars over the windows, when we hardly knew the way ourselves.

On Seeing Bruegel's "Big Fish Eat Little Fish"
Gary Harrison

It happens with the incisive snap of a jaw
Or with the speed of a sharp knife, splitting the flesh—
A splint of steel making an X of the eye,
Like those of hapless fish hanging from hooks in Disney cartoons.
The Old Master saw it clear:
The engorged gullet and belly spilling the day's catch,
A grotesque heap of nested predators—
Big fish stuffed with small, small with smaller.

Across the bay, the city readies its evening orgy of eating.
On the docks and in the kitchens knives flash and gleam.
Strong hands scrape away at scales and skins; heads fall,
The glint of the living eye forgotten in the thin filets laid out
on death beds of steaming rice.

In the chain of being, what is a fish but a hungry mouth with fins?
What is a man but a hungry fish with a knife?

Manhattan
Raymond Johnson

Gut the buildings,
rebuild reuse. Let structures stand
while we are moved with confidence
of simple lines
and time-stressed cornerstones.

Gentrifiers, window washers,
suspended pulley scaffold
on granite face.
Workingmen look down
on hurried crowds and turnstiles.
Around and around angled walls,
rushing down concrete walks,
waist high trash in tall
consuming edifice
of New York City.

Garden here   there
heads bent down toward winter.
Cold gray skies funnel river wind,
sending shivers, waking
a sleeping summer.

On a small round hill
to drink in what bare places
still exist,
in a city jostling for space
and memory's breath,
we look for more or less
a reason.

What I Hold
Hank Blackwell

Heart wants for peace
sacred space
yearning for love to be my will.
Orbits about sun
more abbreviated;
time is the essence.
The days available
for risk and wonder
now most noticeably fewer.
Old heart,
scarred by life's betrayals,
refuses to capitulate.
Wounded, it is wiser
and I, more trusting
this gentle,
loyal companion...
Beauty found with pain
in candle-lit meeting place.
Miles have worn me,
limitations now
the accumulation
of earlier adventures.

Now content to partner
this soul in the choreography
of life's current moments...
Older, I have found respite
in the honesty of observation.
I do not have precious time
to disappoint myself.
Many dark nights,
sorrow and pain
leading me to wake,
grateful
for sunrise, birdsong,
embrace of
family and friend.
All failures
lead to here:

the absence of malice
in my shortcomings
never once separated
me from the heroism
of my children.

APRICOTS
Wayne Lee

the sweet reek of apricots
rotting on the sidewalk

the ache for all that is fallen
and wasted

dry toast growing cold
on his plate

as he stares at her chair

Wolf Print
Wayne Lee

—for Lobo, after "Silent Sentinel,"giclée print from
  watercolor on gouache, Karen Ahlgren, 2017

I try to hold his amber gaze,
but realize I am not animal enough.
He sees through me like canines
rending tendon, muscle and flesh.

Reluctantly I bow to the power of wolf,
to the wild heart that was driven
from the forest of my soul so long
ago, until I surrendered to ferocity

and all that was left behind was cold,
dried blood on snow. But I will rise
again, more beautiful and amazing,
a man standing upright on all four feet.

Rose's Kitchen
Jim Brown

Jake the Rake stopped by Rose's house
to inquire about the gunshot
he had heard early that morning,
found her in the kitchen, naked (except for her boots)

and spattered with blood, a butcher knife
in her fist, a deer's hind quarter
on a plastic tarp on the floor,
her eyes wild. She waved the knife at him.

Don't just stand there gawking, she spat,
go get the rest of it out of the canyon!

Backtracking the blood trail
he had no difficulty finding the carcass,
rolling it into another tarp, slinging it
over a broad shoulder. Scrambling out
of the canyon he smiled to himself,
remembering her sanguinated

sixty year-old body, Barbarella-trim,
leaning over a hunk
of half-skinned venison
on the kitchen floor.

EPIPHANY
David Johnson

There's not a day
that I'm not amazed
by God's excess.

Yesterday
birds filled every branch
of our apple tree.

Today
a young friend
had her womb removed.

Brown Bag Special

Christopher Jaros

I got the deluxe order
a portal in my chest
33 burn jobs and six brown bag specials.

7 a.m. radiation
then a short walk to the lab.

Good results you get the brown bag special
low platelets or white cells and it's see you next week.

Then a short walk to the infusion center
for a couple of hours
of clear bags of solutions and steroids
before the brown bag special.

I make it clear to whoever
brings my lunch
it must be in a white bag.

Half-wild
Wayne Lee

We stood for hours at our neighbor's kitchen window
and watched the woods beyond his yard for any sign
of the bobcat—or half-bob, half-tabby, as Carl claimed
it was. Some days we waited long past dusk to see
if the creature would creep through the tall grass
to steal a bite from the bowl of Alpo Carl left
beneath the big-leaf maple tree.

One black afternoon when we got home from school
an ambulance sat parked in Carl's driveway, its red
hot light spinning in the drizzle. Carl moaned
like a dog hit by a truck and cried out "Mom!"
then leapt from the school bus steps, threw his violin
against the picket fence and raced inside.

I never did see the bob, but I always believed Carl
that one summer eve it took the food, then crouched
in the tree and from the lowest branch dropped silent
as death on the neighbor's Pekinese and sank its fangs
like a wild reminder deep into the fat of its little neck.

WATERBIRD
Raymond Johnson

—for Allen Hunter

Bluer than desert sky,
miles and miles of barren shore,
the choppy high crest manmade lake
is home to the proud-breasted heron.
From a high craggy ledge
where winds carve dolphin face cliffs,
swoops the heron in blue
down to the bass and bluegill,
to the rolling of the manmade lake.

What place my friend had reached
before delivered
to moon's fevered pitch!
How deep the arrow's plunge!
The earth in whose shadow
full moon turned
was more the richer,
having cradled him in his long years.

Taunted by death to leave life aside
we sit the slanted cliffs, waiting with heron,
making waves' pounding
our young hearts' sounding board.
Choppy blue-eyed lake lures the heron
from its windblown home,
as the young are left alone
with the flight of those before.

STRANGE CALM II
Gary Harrison

(March 2020: Shutdown)

The tedious drone
Of traffic and trade
Is muted now
A strange calm
Besets the city
Stilled by fear

At mid morning
A roadrunner's clack
Robin songs
Dove elegies
Regale the ear
As never before.

Dexter's tenor
Chet's trumpet
Heard from the garden
Winter arugula
Baby spinach
We'll need them

Mid afternoon
Fading crocus
Cups of daffodils
Fists of tulips
Soft pink phlox
Stir in the spring wind
A siren wails
To remind us
Families shelter
Ears tuned
The tell-tale cough
A throated rasp
Eerie inquietude

CURRENT

Hank Blackwell

I resist the urge
to hide beneath grassy ledges
like trout my father would find
in high meadow streams.
Life does not always move
to confluence.
It may separate
due to the smallest feature
or nudge from topography.
It is then
that it is best to be the trout
grateful for the current.

ENCOUNTER
Raymond Johnson

Swing of being circling the moment
meeting a monstrous confusion.
Gripped and taken
to a mountain base,
you peer and wonder.
Step past pondering,
hands ready, hands relaxed.

Avalanches some start or caused
by stones tumbling
under fate's mysterious step.

To endure beyond closed eyes,
to forego natural breath.

Forward freedom,
doer thinker.

WHY FISHERS GO TO SEA
Wayne Lee

Spud swears he'll stay sober this trip.
Sven pours pepper on his food until everything
on his plate is black as a freshly tarred net.
Hoot at seventy-two still lives at home
with his invalid mother, still asks her permission
to go out with the boys for a drink after work.
Scooter claims to have bagged the biggest bluefish,
terrapin and barracuda ever recorded in Florida.
Jigs brings along his 30-aught-6 because
he promised his Lummi wife a sealskin coat.
Bud cruises alone when he gets in port
because he says women always travel in pairs
and he likes to take his pick. When the Misty Maid
ties up in Hoonah, the crewmen shower, shave,
comb their hair and douse themselves in Old Spice.
They shine their street shoes, dress in their best
civvies and head up the pier to the only bar in town
to buy each other rounds of CC & water, chase
Native tail and tell the same old stories, leaving out
the part about their dreams.

First Swim
Wayne Lee

Sprinting barefoot down the plank-slick dock,
I dive awkward off the rigid board. I break the gray-
green surface, plunge down to where the water grows
cold as snowmelt, deep as uncle's baritone, down
to where the big trout lurk, where lungs burn, eyes bulge,
scrotum draws taut as a drumhead.

Late that afternoon, small and naked in the bathhouse steam,
confined within its sweating walls and puddled concrete
floor, my skin flushes pink from drying off. I sit on a corner
bench and shiver in my Davy Crockett towel, transfixed
by the monster cocks on the gorilla-haired men.

LATHANDRIA
Raymond Johnson

What of the way she left
dressed darkly and quiet?
Words that filled the long last hour like sunlight
falling in the corner and Lathandria,
soft, pensive, careful,
holding my hand on that faraway day.

Red and gold like fire's glow
the sun was setting. The past,
bowing like a cypress,
the silence of holding on.

Some drown when the sea swells and heaves,
when the earth opens, some plunge.
Ice coats the first of Spring and Summer,
standing broad and challenged,
shivers under the sun's chilled hand.

Not for the healing of defeat
was the longing to embrace so cherished.
Nor could love forestall our youthful
ambition running wild and free
on a windy shore.
You to the sunny south, I to the misty north.

So was this brow soothed and cleansed
while Summer seasoned our harvest of passion.
The robe that covered our hunger
clung to your sweating breasts while you ran
toward the young night and I,
resting and waiting
for my brothers to plunge,
submerge in wet solitude and accept,
like Lathandria,
the sunset, the freedom.

A Northern Soul
David Johnson

Perhaps you are like I am
    with faith in the ancient text
    those quiet conversations with history—
    the measure of print and page.

But we know there are shadows outside
    where god is a dervish dancing
    bears circle the blackberry and
    lovers are known by the way they feel.

Mexican Pharmacy
David Johnson

We'd been careful with food and water—even peeling
   the apples. It was futile.

Women in the market gave baby Sarah whatever
   brightened her blue eyes—
      pieces of pineapple, strawberries.

And at last a bellyache. Two trips to the farmacia
   for aspirin that tasted right—orange-flavored
      rather than lime.

In front of me a peasant girl pleaded with the druggist,
   as if words could dissolve the demons
      consuming her infant.

What kind of bottled miracle did he have for this wasted
   body, all angular—a newborn
      sparrow nuzzling mother's breast.

Sadly, he shook his head and a shadow settled
   around us–it was too late for pills
      and potions.

Turning to leave she gently took her son's bony arms
   and wrapped them like toothpicks in her rebozo.

*And in the memory of our laughter, as it
always has, will wait in darkness
with a timeless patience to bond us one day
to another stranger.*

Chuck Cockelreas

JOY AND LAUGHTER

The Day Before Christmas
David Johnson

In the early morning, garbagemen and I laugh at my old fashioned
suitcoat pulled up to my ears. The cathedral's twin steeples turn pink.

The elegant fronds of the palm trees are silver in the first light.
Blue and white buses begin to rumble like bass drums.

Vendors move towards the plaza. Cobs of buttered corn roast
on a charcoal grill. The air is flavored with deep-fried churros, sugar
and cinnamon, baked sweet potatoes, chile and tacos.

The day begins with such promise, stretches and unwinds. In a chorus
of horns and bleats, the old goatman chases his herd across the intersection
waving a stick and shouting "Putas! Putas!"

With his crippled leg, Eduardo half-walks, half-hops and skips,
his good leg does double-duty. Together we walk twice as fast to show
he is equal to any kid his size. He guides me to special shops, special
prices for me at Christmas time.

We visit the Nacimiento in the central square, life-size figures of
Mary and Joseph on their knees, sheep, burros and shepherds—waiting
as Mexico itself waits, for the transformation of suffering into hope.

Eduardo tugs at me to bend over, then whispers and points to the manger covered with lace that shimmers like spun gold. Tomorrow morning, he says, holding tight to my hand–En la mañana, the crib will no longer be empty. His eyes grow large and glisten like two ornaments.

Eduardo doesn't know that for me the miracle has already happened.

LITTLE CLOWN
Christopher Jaros

My daughter is convinced
she's Little Orphan Annie
wearing a red clown wig
and tons of costume jewelry
as she scurries across the hardwood floors
to send me off to do her bidding.

As Daddy Warbucks leaves the room
he looks back and she appears
in all the beveled edges of each
of the twenty beveled panes
smiling on forever.

Winter Solstice, El Vallecito
Tim Burns

This sleeping meadow—
dreams of spring grass and flowers
under a brilliant white blanket,
its patient life rhythm
pulses slow as a season
in deep and abiding stillness.
The night ocean will soon rise
and swell, its high tide of
blackness spreading steadily across
ridges and meadow on this,
the longest night.

Tonight we shall sing for the sun's
return, drum in praise of life's longing
for itself, and join our dreaming
with the waiting seeds of spring.

Topless on Santorini
David Johnson

I am not used to it, the sight of bare breasts on a beach.
　　I try not to stare while I stare. I wonder if I am obvious.

On Samos, three generations of Swedes unveiled—from baby
　　to grandmother—an exposure of politics as well as freedom.

Every summer, amazons from the north head south to the sea,
　　eager to cast off shame and look lust in the eye.

Up and down the coastline, breasts pointed at the buttery sky,
　　mounds, tepees, small hillocks, loaves of bread—

Pumpernickel, rye, French baguettes, whole wheat, sesame –
　　baking and basking in the sun.

We're all pagans here, worshiping the old gods and goddesses –
　　sun and rain, moon and mountain, sea and desert.

Our bodies were meant to touch other bodies. The reason for nerve
　　endings, fingertips, the delicate surface of our tongues.

The world is brighter, more colors from the rainbow, when sparks
　　leap from my lover's eyes like the Fourth of July.

Big, Loud Toys
Mike Ball

Hundreds of feet high
in a tower-crane cab swivel chair,
and likewise close to the brown and red dirt
in the seat of a motor grader,
smudged and sinewy operators
remain little kids...puerile.

When I and likely you were wee,
we went "Whee!" and "Vroom"
and we roared as we pushed Tonka
dozers and diggers.

If we had grownups to help plan
and build our Erector-set projects,
toys of aggravating bolts and nuts,
we just spoke, well, childish noises.

Know here and now, big boys pushing
the long levers topped with round, black knobs
and twisting the huge steering wheels
make the same noises, grinning all the while.

Service Husband
Wayne Lee

Austin is perfect at *give*, *go in* and *get*.
He practices daily his *push*, *pull* and *alert*.
He understands *unload* the dryer,
pick up the pencil and *fetch* me the phone.

What he can't do is empty the waste
baskets, locate your glasses, or balance
your checking account. He hasn't yet
mastered the fine art of scrubbing

the bathtub or rubbing the small
of your back. For that, and all other tasks
that require opposable fingers and thumbs,
you have at your beck what you only half-

jokingly call me: your service husband. *Sit*,
you sometimes say before dinner. *Speak*,
you implore when you want me to finish
your sentence. *Rise*, you command in bed.

PARADISE
David Johnson

A North American opens the gate to the El Dorado
Trailer Park, and says, "Welcome to paradise." He speaks
the truth. After hundreds of miles sucking up the fumes of Pemex
gas trucks we have arrived safely in heaven, we might not leave.

We bathe in the purple light of evening, like large corks
gently bobbing in the sensuous swells. Our claims to status and rank
dissolve in the warm salt water. We are once more our bodies floating
in the womb.

We talk. "Where you from?" "Where you going?" Manzanillo?
San Blas? What about chiggers? Margaritas in fishbowls?
Does your van ping on the gas?

Road Warriors have a common lexicon of suffering and sensuality.
We follow Odysseus with little regard for answers, so far south
beyond information or truth, maps or memories.

It is simply the caress of the human voice from fellow travelers,
birds flying around in our heads.

SEX IN SCOTLAND
David Johnson

We had come too far north of England to really enjoy the body.
  The Johns had preceded us—Calvin and Knox.

Flesh is rather scarce on the sidewalks of Aberdeen, in buses
  or pastry shops, behind bookshelves—no mini-skirts here.

The incarnate Scotland hides behind closed doors—their fondness
  for beige and gray, practical fibers, simple styles.

Sex is doubtless against the law—a dark thing creeping under
  the pews of empty churches, like the stains left by seagulls.

The youth save their juice for dreaming of a sun baked beach
  in the south—Oh, to wake up naked in someone's arms.

A Song of Joyful Silence
David Kuenzli

I am one with the River as it courses through my veins.
I am one with the Sunlight
That helps to heal my pain.

I am one with the Wind as it blows across my face.
I am one with the Clouds
As they paint the sky with grace.

I am one with Eagle's Wings as they beat within my chest.
I am one with Eagle's Courage
To face life's greatest tests.

I am one with Eagle's Eye as it sees life's deeper worth.
I am one with Eagle's Balance
As he flies between Sky and Earth.
I am one with Mother Nature.
I am one with it all!
In my oneness with all Nature, at last my Soul gives birth
To a song of joyful silence
For our precious Mother Earth.

The Dust of Mexico
David Johnson

"There is a saying that once the dust of Mexico has settled on your heart there can be no rest for you in any other land."

In the Autumn, when the geese honk overhead going south, I spread my feathers and follow the sun.
Just to slip over the border, like sloughing off my clothes.

No matter how many times I've made this crossing, it is ever the first time. A smile creeps into my feet, they begin to tap.
The seams leak and starch runs out of my shirt.

Northwest of Guaymas is San Carlos, where the Sonoran Desert unrolls like a carpet to the edge of the sea. Jagged, razor-back mountains.
The clear skeleton of mesa ringed by fifty miles of light.

On the dry hillsides, scrub, saguaro cactus, lizards doing pushups.
God-like gulls with black trim tilt along the horizon.
In the evening, blues and purples wash across the dunes and rock.

We stand on the beach with one foot in water, the other on shore—
both dry and wet, one extreme touches the other.
Licking salt from our lips, saltwater running through our veins.

Mona and I are king and queen of a patch of tents and children's
toys, castles and towers that wash out with the waves.
There is no other place we'd rather be, nothing is missing.

We envy no one–their condos in Hawaii, chalets in the Alps.
The very best time of our lives. With our family, the circle
is complete. Always today. Today, always.

In some part of my dreams, I walk this beach every night
in the transparency of scented air,
talking with pelicans and seagulls, listening to waves hit the sand.

Only the memories of the crows remain,
their shining shadows large as prehistoric
birds against the redness of the rocks.
At last light, their black, ungainly wings
drive them into the fragile fragments
of the sun, into the chilling blanket
of the night.

Chuck Cockelreas

THE UNINVITED IMAGE

Something About My Father
Levi Romero

something he said to me
that I recalled today

it was not in the shape of his words
or in the language that he used
for he had mastered those well

but rather it was in the way
the tears glazed his eyes
and did not leave the surface
of the pupil

and there at the end

I had learned somehow
to read that look
and come to realize then
that it had not always been
from a night of too much drinking

that look
hard and tarnished like old silver

my father
beautiful man

who had mastered his tears
there at the end

where words had no value
or a warranty that came

with promises unkept

Holding Off on the Day
Scott Wiggerman

Crickets, cicadas,
bugs banging at the screen door,
sounds that break the mesa's silence.

Cool night air not yet replaced
by heat that will press us to shut up
the house, attune our day
to the pulse of air conditioning.

This is the time of appreciation,
the morning sensed through closed eyes,
a time when the world enters
through two small chasms
and can be anything we imagine.

HOMELESS
Ray Johnson

When day's done on the black hour edge,
tired feet from pavement approach,
you rest and reflect
how the old one sleeps
on the crowded streets
far from hills and forest.
Starlings crowd the sky there
where air is moist and sweet.

Alone the old one wakes
in the dark hours.
Food from hands and cans.
Starlings sleep in the reaching maple
high above the Hudson.

There is truth in homelessness
where, uprooted, the maple falls
and starlings disappear at twilight blue.
The old one resting returns to hills
and ponders the world's riches
with one deep breath.

WREN
Hank Blackwell

Staccato welcome
echoes up canyons,
varnished sandstone,
ancient river-wood
now turned to stone.
Waking ancients,
racing raven down canyon
to fertile deltas
holding cholla and scallion.
Centuries move on;
your song has not,
leading
to sacred places
worshipped many songs ago...

MEDITATION: NEW MEXICO BACKYARD
Scott Wiggerman

The muted time as day begins. The cool.
The hummingbirds alone—but also wrens
and mourning doves, and unknown avians.

The bumblebees that shift like molecules.
The corkscrew willows, mountain juniper,
vanilla-scented ponderosa pines.

The coral yuccas, scarlet trumpet vines.
The mint that greens, fans out, overpowers.
The spines of cacti attracting light. The rocks
and paving stones that anchor paths and beds.

The filaments of spiders, things unsaid,
unseen. The timid bunny with white socks.
Give nature praise, and all the natural.
Exalt the morning. Laud the miracle.

Our House in Tlaquepaque
David Johnson

We rented a house on a cobblestone street, swept clean
in the first light by old women in gray rebozos.

Evenings the mariachis called for a Mexican opera, the plaza
filled with dark beauties, wives flowered into lace mantillas.
The click of sequined heels, the snap of fingers.

Muchachos and muchachas slowly circled in opposite directions,
in the shadows stood unforgiving fathers with old watches for eyes.

Tiny flashes of lightning skipped through the trees, farmers burning
 the corn stubble and winter trash, fire in the fields.

Anything was possible, friends might suddenly become lovers.

HAIKU
Jonathan Driscoll

New Mexico autumn
back porch feeders jammed with birds
headed for Miami

hiking snowy ruins
questions and pot shards
everywhere still

BEAR
Hank Blackwell

knowing our slow move
toward slumber,
startled us with
confident cadence.
Turned head
and steady gaze,
drawing us away
from the hypnosis
of evening campfire,
the very moment of autumn
illuminated upon her back.

EVENING PRAYER
Christopher Jaros

The flight of birds at dusk
lingering sun and one evening star
the comfort of twilight.

Night air rushes to the hill
large cranes fly in the distance
turning into waves against the horizon
faster than my eye can follow.

I mumble a silent simple prayer.

WELCOME TO DYSTOPIA
Tim Burns

The clouds! The clouds!

Roiling surges and melding, blending fractals
held by the vast cerulean sky;
the whitest white, thrilling shades of gray.
Ocean-like waves (am I underwater?) crash overhead;
Chaos of the most sublime disordered order

But wait
What's this?

No, it cannot be;
I'm hallucinating, cast, in a blink of the eye, into the hell realms,
And no Virgil to guide the way.

There is no refuge, no quarter has been spared.

The sacred displays itself in unfathomable ways.

Familiar Face

Hank Blackwell

My father sleeps fitfully,
white whiskers shading his pain.
I am not ready for his face;
I have not yet earned it ...

Raven Etiquette
Jim Brown

I crept silently—or so I thought—to the edge
of a basalt-rimmed canyon to investigate
the odd sounds coming from somewhere below,
leaned
ever—so—slowly
to peer over the rim,

saw a pair of ravens perched
on a ledge ten feet below, facing out, discussing,
it seemed to me, something of great interest.
As my head cleared the rim (nobody
was ever quieter than I was, looking over that rim),
they stopped their conversation.

One glanced up at me over its shiny black shoulder,
evidently un-alarmed, for neither one flew from the ledge.
They just shut up.

When our time comes,
we give ourselves away
a box of memories at a time, a bag of
emotions, a notebook of observations,
a collection of conclusions –

Chuck Cockelreas

I GROW OLD

I Grow Old
Jonathan Driscoll

—for Joseph Woods

fishing the canyons and forests
of New Mexico
that simplest and best
of ancient Daoist pleasures

in the deep space of one man
natural, free, and flowing
are all mountains and rivers

EN ROUTE
Raymond Johnson

Road stretched forth
to the day's reach,
through timber and barren hills
while you rest with eyes half closed,
content with the fallen hours
and long long, look toward sunset.

These your sojourning days
living off vistas and manners
of a thousand years.

Take the Clothes

Mike Ball

Ah, my naughty great-uncle.
Alone among eight siblings and spouses,
in not keeping his trousers zipped.
(That would be the seventh commandment.)

The necrology reports he died at home.
The coroner could dispute that.
Sudden death in the upbeat atop
a mistress is too exotic for our staid family.

The missus shielded his honor and kept his corpse close,
mingling under a shared headstone 30 years later.
Passion for the German war bride faded to the quotidian
then betrayal dissolved with him in the ground.

When the box with 14 ritzy shirts came
to my steps by surprise, I knew to ask
his niece, my mother, why these came to me.

My mother did not sigh often
yet she was skilled at it and said.
"Gerty did not want to keep his clothes,
shirts he might have worn with HER.
She still would not throw parts of him away.
Take the damned shirts and write a thank-you note.
Then do whatever you want to with them.
She will never mention the shirts again.
She has cleared those bureau drawers and her mind."

I heard, "Our wants are trivial
weighed against what another needs."

OLD DOG
Hank Blackwell

Gray at the muzzle,
slow to rise
with the arthritis
of many runs,
and skirmishes.
Growling at
those who would
scratch scarred ears,
escaping through open gates
away from warm meals—
loving company.
Barking at neighbors,
chewing shoes and
chair legs...

Yet, you remain,
unconditional, patient.
Old dog returns,
gratefully circling
the worn pillow
at your feet...

GIFTS TO GEEZERS
Mike Ball

In the brown, open field, three score plus 10
waxy stalks remain following harvest.
Here though, the rich soil is really frosting
and all those dripping stalks are lit candles.

So many flames emit great light, prompting
jests of triggering the smoke alarm. Ho!
The tedium of these wee lights, suggests
using a big 7 and 1 next year.

The psalmist fixed the days of all our years.
Now small gifts appear, like no jury duty.
Fishing and hunting licenses are free.
Living long has earned rewards for them.

70 is not through a mythic arch
of dragons or angels' wings. Rather, we
walk our local path and suddenly pass
into this new land of the hoary haired.

The septuagenarian trail, in fact,
has no map on a signpost to guide us.
There is neither mile marker nor warning.
We are young, then lo we are 70.

Balancing Act
Scott Wiggerman

So it's back to this:
the spine suspended from the body
like a hanger that's been bent back
to its original shape one too many times.

The medicated menthol scent of ointments
on the shirts and sheets, strong enough
to coat the tongue with its proximity.

That awkward stance of
bending without bending,
of putting on pants or socks,
of walking in slow-mo.

The hours of standing upright against walls,
pushing between the L3 and L4 with fists,
of never quite finding the spot.

It comes back—
the physical therapy, the appointments,
the acupuncture, the epidurals—

and there's no willing it away:
the crumpled spine,
the only thing on the mind.

Stretched across a bed
in the middle of the afternoon,
playing dead, the fear of shifting
from a position of relative relief,

aware the slightest adjustment
will bring another wave of pain.
This balancing act toward comfort.

Remembering the spry times—
cartwheels, somersaults, Twister—
of a body from another lifetime,
of a mind that never imagined
the unjust injuries of aging.

Love, Share and Live!
David Kuenzli

Feel into the Wisdom, the Wisdom from your tears.
Embrace and share the Wisdom from your creative aging years.
Find a deeper Purpose in the midst of all your pain.
See beyond what seems to be to the love there in between.

Hairs
Christopher Jaros

I dreaded going down to the basement.
Sitting on stool and waiting
for the sound of the clippers to start.

How many times will he say sit still
before my hairs litter the floor.

Someday I will pay to have my hair cut.

I grew up and had kids of my own.
I never cut a single hair.

Around the time my father turned 90
he asked me to give him a buzz cut.
Now when I go to visit him
I start to dread where we are in the hair cutting cycle.

I gave myself a buzz cut
before I started chemo and radiation

OH

Hank Blackwell

Forgetful,
values rearranged
fly open, unshaven several days
youthful injuries alighting
like Hitchcock's birds
on joints and jar-opening
fingers....
Elders never shouted
or whispered warnings,
let us laugh and wonder
about changing gaits
wrinkled clothing,
knowing we would arrive
rapidly upon these
bittersweet evenings

An RV Park in the Yucatan

David Johnson

Harry often sits in the open cockpit of his motorhome
and talks down to the rest of us on his RV pad,
like a World War II pilot leaning out of his B-25 bomber
to talk to comrades on the runway.

Harry is not an attractive person. Somehow he has lived
his entire life without a hint of transcendence.
Back in the States, we would have left him to his misery.
But Mexico has touched us and we listen to his loneliness,
the sad hymns of mortality.

As he tires, his phrases are strung out on small puffs
of air, as if his severely impaired lungs were saying goodbye.
"I came back, the same doctor, here in Merida. Put me on
some pills, said it's not too late."

We pull our chairs a little closer, forming a half moon
around Harry, waiting for some dark, earthy song
from Harry's body, like the conch shell blown by a Mayan
priest when he opens the chest and uncovers the heart.

Harry will die soon and, because he is human, he deserves
some sonorous fanfare to send him across with his fishing rod.

There was no glimpse
of future then,
only bright and floating
sparks that climbed
the dark sky and winked
out among the stars.

Chuck Cockelreas

BE GENTLE, BE KIND, BE STRONG

THE UNFINISHED ROAD
Stewart Warren

I must go, says the man,
before my spirit dies.
A road trip is born.
He yearns for choices determined
by weather, by watershed
and the flow of clouds descending
into a mountain town.
He will eat and pray
and wink when he wants,
though mindful
not to add anything extra.

The open road is so named,
and nothing real can be dodged.
Love, neither judging nor invested,
takes the reins of every wind,
leads where it will.
So you see, he's actually a follower,
a devotee of change.
He's straight out for the desert.
He writes these things to remember.
Talk of tests and treatments
fade into a dusty sunset west of Van Horn.
It's a choice on the road.

The ways of the world
have their demands,
and so too the spirit.
Wyoming or not,
the sun comes and goes
at the pleasure of its pulse,
and time, that darling dream,
loses its incremental edges
at the persistence of beauty.

A man writes
an unfinished poem on the banks
of a shifting river somewhere
west of Steamboat Springs.
Doubt keeps him clean
and all that is present
has been chosen by love.

CRADLE & WOMB
Tim Halford

They say a man lived here once,
constant Water
flowing by,
and in,
and under,
his Abode.

His days
must have been
filled with hunting for food,
firewood for cold nights
while planning for
the next day.

And when that was done,
He sat with the Grandfathers
all around him
Wisdom whispering Truth
in the overhead branches.

Other tree brothers
stood by his side,
a kind Camaraderie
under blue skies.
Sun setting
Creek rippling,
Wind blowing,
Birds chirping
Constant Chorus.

At night,
and when
the weather changed,
always Welcoming,
was Cave Mother

Nestled in her
stony loving arms,
safe, warm,
nurturing,
peaceful sleep.

Perhaps that is all
we really want
To Hold
and be Held,
To Love
and be Loved,
Safely,
Unconditionally.
Accepted.

In our Natural
imperfect perfection
a refuge,
along the
returning path
towards Home.

CYCLIC MOVE
Raymond Johnson

I knew a woman who thrived on touch
and merged at the flesh of day.
A treasure it was to
lie with her.
Then time made a precious move
and lunged at the point of closeness.
Now we stand in light, wantless of love,
between blossoms and a peerless sky.

Framing Father's Flag
Tim Halford

A triangular frame,
Seen flags in them a thousand times,
Easy to install, hang it on the wall.
Yet I could not get it to fit right
As I unfurled, refolded, and set it inside,
Maybe fifty times,
Folded and creased this way and that way,
into that restrictive, perfect frame.

It just did not feel right.
Frustration, tears,
Now I am suddenly out there
Swimming,
in the Deep.
Don't give up.

Only the white stars
on the blue background
didn't fit for my Father.

There needed to be blood red,
The risk that came with the war to end all wars,
the birth of his new generation,
the loss of wife and a son,
too, too soon.
Deep wounds come from
endings you can't see coming.

Yes, also blue for wide open skies,
white stars in the night of his boyhood dreams,
great accomplishments in his life,
battles won,
and the deep blue griefs
that held him close to himself,
so often,
alone.

A white stripe,
genuine innocence
a lifetime of service to others,
pockets of joy, love, divinity
and now,
perfect peace.

Folding, unfolding, unfurling,
I thought of how I was there,
And wasn't,
for him.
What was,
what could have been,
how I wish he were here
with me now.

Suddenly through a
tearful smile
I see a refolding,
Against the creases,
And the reframing
of our shared life.

What flag will be framed for me?
What colors and what stories?
How will it be framed?
And from whose wall will it hang?

However these are answered,
He will be there
in my blood red
blue sky,
white-starred, story
he witnesses from afar.

La Vida es un Tango
Juan Velasco

One needs to learn, watch, try and perfect.

The secret is your inner self y la pareja con quien compartes.

Por ahora, dream of flores y lluvia, children playing y un viejo caminando
con su bastón.

Hora de estar presente y deja los viejos cuentos y repeated complaints.

You have made a living y ahora es cuando la vida es lo que das.

Tienes la responsabilidad de compartir and may others know the real you.

More smiles and laughter - more ice cream and cake.

Tus hobbies will keep you alive y el atardecer te abrirá el corazon.

Escucha el cantar de los pájaros, the smell of rain, and be aware de la agonía
de los pobres y less fortunate.

Give bottom up - que necesitas. Not top down - tienes que.

La vejez = old age = learning to dress standing up, cook simple y un buen
vaso de vino.

Estar afuera con aire puro and where the senses which still work give you all.

The sun will set soon and learn to have amigos y comunidad around you

Eso es todo - mañana no existe.

My Grandfather's Hands
Vittorio La Cerva

My Grandfather's hands were peasant ones: big and strong, and
always dressed in callouses or cuts or blackened nails.

They were helping hands, kind ones that held me softly with
encouragement, never with violence or malice.

Satisfied with simple pleasures of family, food, friends, never grasping
for more more more.

They were not particularly skilled—no fine carpentry or luxurious
gardens came of them.

His day job was transporting prisoners for the NYC police department,
which he supplemented with delivering Western Union telegrams
and candygrams in Brooklyn ghettos. He laid out the route and
drove through desolate landscapes, while I climbed grimy flights
of stairs, and trudged through garbage and urine-soaked hallways.
My first intense exposure to the wider world of suffering, as
trembling hands took a telegram that reeked of death or other
bad news or shook with joy at receiving a special treat for Easter or
Mother's Day.

He never left or entered the house without touching my grandmother
gently and asking, "how is my darling today?"

As he aged, his hands just became more so. All the love and caring
that emanated from them were evident as he held my children,
ate a favorite meal or tinkered on piano or mandolin.

In the vastness of the world, they remained a steady presence of love,
a paradigm of masculine goodness.

I was blessed to hold them one last time, as he took his last ahhhhhh
into eternity, the sweetest sound I've ever heard.

THE MAGICIAN
David Kuenzli

My life is much more than what it seems
When Magician unlocks my deeper dreams.

In the sacred place between time and space,
My life transforms from the commonplace.
My life is so much more than what I perceive
When I open my mind and my heart to receive.

YEARS AFTER MY FATHER DIED
Levi Romero

and his body was lain into the earth
his garden continued to yield vegetables
radishes and carrots burrowed into the dark
moist dirt and the onion stalks stood straight
as the soldiers standing for the twenty-one gun salute

yesterday morning crickets purred
under the shade of the last broad
green leafed plant in the yard
while insects flicked under a canopy
of morning glories

last time I saw you
we spoke of conflict
and that all endings
must have resolution

this afternoon I long
for the voice of the
red breasted robin

I yearn for the slow sinking rhythm
of a long summer evening
and good conversation

a thin thread of web glistens
in the crook of the plum tree
I am accompanied only
by the caw and swooping flight
of the crow across the afternoon sky

the sunflowers in the meadow
are crowned with halos of petals
browned and golden in the haze
of autumn sunlight
crouched and looking
like old men
with wrinkled faces

their reach toward the sun

frozen in a final grasp
toward warmth and light

FACE TO FACE

David Johnson

A leper sat taking the sun in the center of the main plaza,
the most direct route from home to the tortillaria.

For days I detoured around him, having just begun to learn
Mexico's lessons about dealing with the contours of reality.

Finally one morning I walked up to the leper and looked at him
straightaway: half of his face was purple jelly, as if one cheek
had begun to melt and drift back towards the ear.

From a small, dark opening used for a mouth--a hole just large enough
for a pencil--a distinctly human voice whispered, "Buenos días."
A wrinkled hand reached out to shake one of mine, and I
felt the warmth of his flesh.

SOUTH OF THE BORDER
David Johnson

Slowly my mask is stripped away. Mexicans don't seem
to care about Martin Luther or Minnesota, whether I leave
my guilt at the border. They're not fooled
by my credentials or credit rating.

No one will accuse me of dishonesty, if I remove my
mask and become myself. Money spills out of my wallet
like seeds. I feel like Adam in the first garden
learning the real names for fruits like naranjas and fresas.

LET SOUL FIND US
Tim Halford

(After *Anam Cara*, The Beginning)

When the
crust of compensation
cloaks around the heart
When the Soul is evicted
by the manic outward.
When moral surgery
excises the truthful
negative within
which
rarely lies to us.
Let Soul find us...

Out from the
courage of solitude
concealed in the silence
between and beyond words,
warmth from the eternal hearth
of the penumbral world
Let Soul Find us...

Shy, playful, childlike
Intimations of the secret truth
whisper:
"Wounds of the Spirit
Always Heal"

Where the darkness is not exiled,
Instead transformed.
Brought home
Soul adores unity.
Let Soul find us...

In the Landscape of surprise
Beauty is found
in the most neglected places.
Destiny then falls into place
Awakens our true rhythm
Brings us providence
Let Soul find us...

then,
and only Then,
My Dear,
I am
Untouchable,
Dashing about
in the landscape of surprise,
A well breaks open
Deep in the center of my chest
An inner belonging
Soul Has Found Me.

Our ancestors are all around me here.
I feel the distant vibrations of the drum
and hear the high, clean voices
of the singers in the wind.

Chuck Cockelreas

THE ROAD AHEAD

Body is in Soul
Tim Halford

Soul
Comes through the back door,
Up from the basement,
Not conjured in a séance,
Invited in by a moral sermon
Or mechanical unfelt repetitive ritual
If asked
in a certain plea
It might come out to play;
in solitude, awkward silences,
when thought has expired.

Soul
Icon of the body
Body
Its public biography
that betrays it.
A Custodian of
deep ancient thresholds,
Sensuous,
Carrying what we feel
Its signature deep inside
The World flows through it
And then out again.

Soul
It knows the person you dream that you are
Not what others expect
The geography of
Your True Destiny
and how You are
to get there.
Its voice guaranteeing
You will not be exiled
from your true Royal
Divinity
Within.

THE UNFAILING FREEFALL

Stewart Warren

The instructions were clear—
disown the world without regret.
Detach the leads and wires
of homespun bondage,
your insistence on cherished
but failed dreams. Unplug.

Icons and schemes vie for your loyalty,
play leapfrog on the grid.
Oh, how they wiggle and shine.
But consider the center first,
the dot.org of your true domain,
a constant reality withstanding.

Go to the park, the café,
the rally, the prison, the mechanic.
Go out on a limb.
You will not have abandoned them.
The good work begins in every now.
Smiling in silence supersedes phenomena.
Smiling in silence
supersedes all phenomena.

Once again the tulips
have reconciled winter,
flaunt their ridiculous beauty.
Your only desire is to love from unity,
to be faithful to the fullness.

We're shown how
to use our hands and words
as purpose unfolds. Everyone is neighbor.
Held securely in boundlessness
the Greatness opens out
from here, the always open
cave of your heart.
Held securely in boundlessness
you step and a thousand bridges appear.

Fin de Semana
Juan Velasco

Fin de semana y no se donde se fue -
   minúsculos que haceres que tratan de llenar un vacío
   un pozo profundo donde hay campo para muchas capas
   la mayoría célebres de algún buen momento y otras amargas
   buenos recuerdos que se disipan en el agua mientras las malas
      flotan como aceite
   lo bueno enterrado como un rayo en la montaña
   lo malo como el trueno que sigue y sigue rebotando de montaña
      en montaña

Lo importante de escribir para que algun dia alguien lo lea y vea
   otra realidad
   recuerdos de alguien que es parte de los que somos
   espejos que reflejan lo que fue y aclara lo que es. Pero no lo que será.
   sonrisas y lágrimas que dicen lo mismo
   unas de felicidad y otras de miedo como en un mar de viento bravo
   con olas en la oscuridad y lluvia que cortan no solo la piel pero
      también la esperanza

Santo mío, qué hemos hecho para destruir tanto bueno
   los atardeceres tan bravos y los amaneceres llenos de esperanza
   el tiempo que debería curar aguas que se llevan tanto al profundo
   cielos azules como el lápiz lazuli, sangre como el rojo del coral
      mediterraneo, y el amarillo que no entiendo,
   mesclalos y te daran tonos de lo que fue y de lo que es posible
   un arcoiris doble del cual soñamos
   rafagas de viento y lluvia que en su fin traen lo mejor

El sol se pone hoy en la montaña a las 5 en punto
cuando de su vuelta, que traiga algo bueno que nos de esperanza

MÖBIUS

Scott Wiggerman

With mystifying twists and turns,
          gravity-defying inclines and declines
                    designed by M.C. Escher

this mountain road goes on
          and on over the same terrain
                    (Haven't I seen that fir before?)

(Haven't I crossed this stream?)
          of endless hills and valleys
                    populated with aspen and pine

tinged in hope and darkness,
          in myriad shades of green,
                    this road of no end

and no beginning—but also
          no markers, no billboards, not
                    a single vehicle or person,

no telephone or power lines,
          nor any hint of civilization
                    other than this road and this car,

which drives itself so
           I can gaze at infinite landscapes
                      teasing every rise and bend,

whether they look like what
           I've seen before or whether
                      they are exactly the same,

stuck on endless replay—
           and isn't that how my life had been
                      before I found the magic of this road?

BORDERS
David Johnson

In the Autumn, when the geese honk overhead going
south, my heart joins them and we follow the sun,
just to slip over the border, like slipping out of my clothes.

No matter how many times I've made this crossing,
it is always the first time.

A smile creeps into my feet and they begin to tap.
The seams leak and the starch runs out of my shirt.

Northwest of Guymas is San Carlos, where the Sonoran
Desert like a sand carpet unrolls to the edge of the sea.

In some part of my dreams, I walk along this Mexican
beach every night, in the transparency of scented air,
talking with the cormorants and frigate birds.

GOODBYE
Raymond Johnson

Wonder not in cloudy sleep
by what you are inspired.
Look and see the leveled tree
and fruiting wonder
of Earth's fragrant fluids.

I will one day die
in the redwoods.
I will be old
like revolution and change.

What better morrow
than when you awake
and walk the open way
into a wash or a ravine?
To one side you will slip,
soon to be forgotten,
you the wash or the ravine.

February in New Mexico
David Johnson

Not miracle as overturning science or reason, raising the dead
    or changing water into wine.

But the miracle of awaking from a dream. Birth is as everyday
    as Canadian geese flying in a flawless vee.

Not super-natural, but nature itself. The life force steals your
    breath, like the shimmer of gold in a field of sunflowers.

Birthing a child is different from staring at stars in the night sky.
    You turn the telescope around, look deep rather than vast.

The eye turned on the mystery within. The elemental rhythm,
    like feeling the drumbeat inside your bones.

The crowning of David James took us to the threshold of spirit—
    flesh of our flesh, creator and creation.

As Maia birthed her son, a chorus of ancestors cheered her on—
    parents, grandparents, uncles and aunts.

Encircled by prayer, an eternal flame lit the core of his being.
    Anointed with his natal waters, each breath a benediction.

Every child is the chosen one, every newborn the messiah.
    This is the gift—Time renewed, darkness transformed into light.

RIVER STONES
Hank Blackwell

Each moment begins,
sharp stone,
fractured from the vein...
falling into swift current
of life's river.
Tumbling with others,
over soft silt
and hardened boulder,
surfaces begin to polish.
Rounded and smooth,
soon similar
one to another
in size and weight.
Finally, arriving home...
tiny, glittering grains
upon the endless beach.

Limbs
Gary Harrison

Lives rest upon such fine limbs.

Sometimes
   the stillness
    of a windless noon,

Sometimes
   the reckless tempest
    of an autumn storm—

We feel it
   all;
    we bear it
     all—
    Sun rise
     sun fall.

On whetted wings
   we rush
    into the crowd,

Trumpeting
   our solitary
    psalms of joy.

Or on still wings
    we glide,
        in utter silence,

Rehearsing our final sentence.

A Miracle on March 17, 7:21 A.M.
David Johnson

I know spring has come too soon
    when young couples sink to the grass
        hang on each other's lips, feeling
            more than ashes below the waist.

It's a serious problem in the Sunbelt–
    not knowing the right season for love or
        death, when to sharpen the scythe,
            when to break all the plates.

Look at California, surfing with Beach Boys,
    an endless trip through a wet tunnel.
        mature men devoted to the ultimate wave,
            forgetting that salmon die after spawning.

ABOUT THE AUTHORS/ARTISTS

MICHAEL BALL

Michael Ball has visited Northern New Mexico many times. His mother spent her last 25 years there and her sister was head nurse at the Indian Hospital for decades. His sister and her husband, daughter and grandson live near Española. To put it crudely, he is a writing slut, from daily and weekly newspapers to technical and business magazines to too many help systems and manuals. Poetry doesn't require apologies for tropes and jokes.

HANK BLACKWELL

A New Mexico native, a father, grandfather, teacher, jeweler, ballet dancer, mountaineer, writer and fire chief, Hank has been involved in New Mexico Men's Wellness for over 35 years, and is the editor of "Man, Alive!", a digital, New Mexico men's publication. The diverse and varied opportunities of observation, gratitude, wonder, crises, emotion, and vulnerability created a diverse recipe for the importance of poetry in Hank's life. His most recent poetry collection is *Silver Chain*.

JIM BROWN

Jim Brown is a retired mind-body specialist and eternal information sponge who lives in Mount Shasta, California. He and his wife Molly were married in Los Alamos in the early 60s, having both grown up there since shortly after the Manhattan Project ended. He has published a prior collection of his poems, and more recently an informative book, *Anatomy of Embodied Education*, co-authored with his long-time Santa Fe friend Tim Burns.

TIM BURNS

Since his auspicious move to northern New Mexico in 1973 as a public-school teacher, Tim has had the great, good fortune of bringing his abiding curiosity about and knowledge of the embodied brain to students and teachers throughout the world. Time with loved ones, creating art, the odd poem and occasional book—blended with outdoor adventure in the company of some amazing men—makes for a rich and truly satisfying life journey.

JONATHAN DRISCOLL

Jon Driscoll lives in the mountains near Pecos, New Mexico. He is a former Buddhist priest who studied in Japan for many years when he was younger. He had his own business as a cross cultural consultant in California. He now does design work and runs the wood working shop at Ten Thousand Waves. Writing poetry has been a compulsion since high school.

TIMOTHY HALFORD

Timothy Halford is a successful entrepreneur and former criminal justice professor at the collegiate level. He has served with the Joseph Campbell Foundation, men's support organizations, volunteer groups and is a proud grandfather and father. His main interest is the intersection of myth and psyche, having designed and hosted a poetry podcast. He has traveled the world and continues to seek new adventures.

ROGER HARMON

While a kid from Western Kansas, summer vacations brought him to New Mexico. The state was indeed the Land of Enchantment and he sought to capture that sense of wonder with the family's Brownie. In 1995, after a decade in Asia, he came to live in Jemez Springs, met his wife Nancy, and moved to Albuquerque. Roger takes photographs almost every day, either on walks with Bravo or on trips to Baja, Mexico, Vietnam, Bhutan and beyond.

GARY HARRISON

Gary Harrison, retired professor of English, taught Romantic poetry, poetics and world literature at UNM for nearly 30 years. During those years, with family and friends, he hiked and backpacked in the canyons, deserts, and mountains of New Mexico. Now retired from academia, he is putting more energy into writing poetry and songs. He has published a monograph on William Wordsworth, numerous articles on Romantic poetry, and, as co-editor, two world literature anthologies.

CHRISTOPHER JAROS

Christopher Jaros was born in Kansas City, Mo. He studied literature at Westminster College and the University of Missouri, K.C. where he received his B.A. in English. He has lived in various locations in the Great Southwest and now resides in Albuquerque where he moved three years ago. He is semi-retired. In his free time, he enjoys hiking, biking, walking, and playing in any card game anywhere. He published the book *Poems, Pictures, and Musings, A Life in Review* last year and continues to be involved in various, artistic endeavors.

DAVID JOHNSON

For over 30 years David Johnson taught Creative Writing and World Literature in the English Department, University of New Mexico. He has participated in and supported the mission and activities of Men's Wellness in New Mexico since 1986. He has been married to Mona for over 50 years, with three wondrous children, Peter, Sarah, and Maia.

Raymond Johnson

New Mexico woodworker and poet Ray Johnson grew up in Milwaukee during the fifties and sixties and earned his BA in Romantic languages from the University of Wisconsin. In the early eighties, he moved to Albuquerque via NYC. For many years, Johnson taught in the Albuquerque Public Schools. A life-long gardener, outdoorsman, craftsman, and furniture maker, Johnson has been writing poetry for over fifty years. Raymond now lives in Rio Rancho, NM. overlooking the Rio Grande valley.

David Kuenzli

David was the leader of the NMMW Fall Conference in 1990 and organized more than 30 men's support groups focusing on ways to become more direct and open about our deeper feelings about the meaning and purpose of our lives. A singer/songwriter of more than 600 songs and 35 recent poems, David is currently working on an album addressing some of the many challenges we face regarding social and racial injustice.

Victor La Cerva

Victor La Cerva, MD, has been celebrating the joys & sharing the challenges of being masculine since NMMW's inception. His wife and two grown daughters consistently inspire him to be a better man. Playing music, into the woods on horseback and wordsmithing always bring him alive. *Letters To A Young Man In Search Of Himself* was a joyful attempt at wisdom sharing. He does a free weekly podcast on matters of importance, myheartsongs.org .

Wayne Lee

Wayne Lee (wayneleepoet.com) lives in Santa Fe. Lee's poems have appeared in Pontoon, Tupelo Press, The New Mexico Poetry Review and other journals and anthologies. He was awarded the 2012 Fischer Prize and has been nominated for a Pushcart Prize and three Best of the Net Awards. His collection *The Underside of Light* was a finalist for the 2014 New Mexico/Arizona Book Award. He is currently working on a full-length collection of septets and a memoir about his years as caregiver for his disabled wife.

Levi Romero

Levi Romero was selected as the inaugural New Mexico Poet Laureate in 2020 and New Mexico Centennial Poet in 2012. His most recent book is the co-edited anthology, Querencia: Reflections on the New Mexico Homeland. His two collections of poetry are *A Poetry of Remembrance: New and Rejected Works* and I*n the Gathering of Silence*. He is co-author of *Sagrado: A Photopoetics Across the Chicano Homeland*.

Uwe Schroeter

Uwe Schroeter has been an active participant in, a leader of, and a photographer of quarterly NM Men's Wellness events since 2005. He is a native of Germany, has worked as an English-to-German technical translator for more than 27 years, and has lived in New Mexico for nearly a quarter century. His leisure pursuits include photography, travel, hiking and yoga, and he often finds that these four combine well.

Juan Antonio Velasco

Born October 1942 in La Paz, Bolivia, Juan has lived in many countries, the USA being home for over 56 years. He has attended several universities (4 degrees), was a Naval Officer during the Vietnam War, a banker in NY and relocated to Santa Fe in 1974. He was in NM State employment 7 years, jewelry business for 25 years, then owned an orchard near Silver City for 12 years, now devoting his life to wood art, immigrants and projects at the border as well as ensuring good food production and assisting at a farm.

Stewart Warren

An impassioned traveler, finding significance and divinity each moment, intimate with darkness, yet reflecting it with love, humor, light, and faith. Stewart used his alchemical process to inspire readers' exploration. Through Mercury Heartlink, he produced 29 of his books, numerous anthologies, and 136 authors. An awakener, provocateur, and mystic, he left a trail of festivals, groups, and fond memories, also a driving force in the creation of the Albuquerque poet laureate program.

Scott Wiggerman

Scott Wiggerman is the author of three books of poetry, Leaf and Beak: Sonnets, Presence, and Vegetables and Other Relationships; and the editor of several volumes, including *Wingbeats: Exercises & Practice in Poetry*, *Bearing the Mask*, *Weaving the Terrain*, and *22 Poems & a Prayer* for El Paso, winner of a 2020 NM/AZ Book Award. He is the Chair of the Albuquerque Chapter of the New Mexico State Poetry Society.

Joseph Woods and Kris Thoeni

Joseph and Kris create visionary art that is inspired by spirit, created with love, and intended to touch your soul. They work side by side to create colorful, whimsical images on silk. Each painting is a collaboration, a tool for transformation and healing. Their work is displayed in hospitals and used in leadership retreats focusing on spirituality and healing.

www.josephandkris.com

www.kristhoeni.com

These gentle, kind, generous poets are also gentle, kind and generous men. This anthology would not have been without their talent and poetic vision. David Johnson and Ray Johnson made this project better, just as they continue to make the world better. With respect, admiration and love, we are ever grateful. Thank you, thank you.

Hank Blackwell

Made in the USA
Middletown, DE
12 October 2021

49714471R00092